THIRD EYE AWAKENING

Discover new Perspectives to open your Third Eye Chakra, through Psychic Awareness, Healing and Meditation. Increases Psychic Abilities purifying your Energy Field

Francis Schulz

TABLE OF CONTENTS

INTRODUCTION

According to Taoism, the third eye, also known as the mind's eye, is located between the two actual eyes and when opened, expands to the center of the forehead. According to Taoism, the third eye is one of the body's primary energy centers, situated at the sixth Chakra, forming a main meridian segment.

This line connects the left and right hemispheres of the body. Consider the third eye as a cone with the small end connected to the forehead and the big end containing the filter.

If you are unaware of how you get and process information, you would have no idea how to rate the information you receive. If you become aware of your observations and insight, it's time to develop an acute sensitivity to the direction in which the sensation leads you and to following directions.

One of the first things you must do is TRUST that you possess everything necessary to comprehend, perceive, extend your consciousness, and act on the wisdom provided to you. The more you trust and react to knowledge, the more it will protect you, assist you in your endeavors, elevate your quest or provide profound transformation.

The third eye has long-range perceptions, future forecasts, and insight into market transactions or patterns. This is also beneficial when scooping information. Again, it requires trusting yourself and the information coming in. Test your information and put into action what is being directed to you to take action.

For the third eye to open and expand, you have to relax as you continue to ask questions. Then with each question, you need to learn to connect to that higher consciousness part of yourself and realize that the information and insight are acceptable and that you can receive the correct information and follow directions to your greater success.

Try tuning in to things before they happen, before the phone rings to see if you get an impression of who will call. If you watch a news program, open yourself to impressions you may get and what if any actions come to mind, read a newspaper, and tune into any specific insights you may receive.

Tune into hunches for new businesses or directions on how to move your business or what trend will be important. Think about a person you know and ask specific questions of your third eye regarding that person and see or hear what impressions may come in. Don't discard visual or audio impressions you may receive.

Keep assuring yourself that you are perfectly fine and that you can stay relaxed. When someone new approaches you, stay as relaxed as possible and listen with your third eye and heart zone.

The first impression is usually the one to tune into. If you are not receiving any impressions during that time, ask yourself if you are blocking or if you aren't open to receiving impressions or if the person is blocking.

Also, keep in mind that the divine provides the means for psychic creation. You should feel confident in your ability to use your third eye and originate from a higher consciousness.

Suppose you become afraid or there are many negative impressions. In that case, you can simply turn it off by saying that you want only the highest vibrations of good and positive energy to enter and that you can respond only to positive energy.

If you feel afraid, distressed, or compelled in a negative direction or feel compelled to harm someone or yourself, understand that this is never coming from your higher consciousness or spiritual self.

Your spiritual self or higher consciousness reacts exclusively to empathy, kindness, and the greatest good for all. It will never direct or order you to harm or compromise another.

Also, the third eye's energy is a weapon of reach and knowledge; you cannot psychically invade someone without their permission. It is not intended to be used as a weapon of any kind. It is mutual respect, empathy, kindness, information sharing, the prevention of loss of life or profits, and a commitment to upliftment.

Continue learning, be receptive to your experiences, and train yourself not to pass judgment on the knowledge you get.

Happy Reading

CHAPTER: 1 YOUR THIRD EYE

The third eye is where long vision is used to access everything. At times, you can experience a column or cone of light reaching forward and outward, just like a beacon of light capturing everything in a way that you need to comprehend. You may get a wealth of knowledge necessary to make an informed decision and to work for the most appropriate approach for someone's healing.

You must develop an awareness of some of the many zones within your body and consciousness. It entails cultivating sensitivity in various receiving areas of your physical and mental ability.

You can move between areas if you become conscious of and tuned into your physical and mental bodies and the environment around them. If you've developed an awareness of your own space, you will develop an awareness of the space surrounding other bodies. You begin to experience the aura fields that surround and exist within all.

When working from the third eye, you must develop an awareness of the sensation of working inside your brain, more in the quarter-size point directly between your brows. There are moments when you feel a sense of pressure and opening. Occasionally, you can become aware of colors or energy changes emanating from that region.

To gain an understanding of a person's emotional condition to create a long-term strategy. Also, working with your third eye enables you to receive direct thoughts or emotions from another being nearby.

The third eye is the primary source of psychic abilities for most people. Consider when you're thinking about a friend and unexpectedly receive a call from her or him.

This association is the third eye area's responsibility. A fantastic concept or technological breakthrough happens almost simultaneously around the globe. This is the third eye gathering the same knowledge accessible to anybody open to it and willing to work with it.

Knowledge Access

You could use the third eye area to gain a more detailed understanding of a project. If a snag or roadblock occurs, simply request clarification, direction, or be seen differently. There are countless methods for accomplishing the same task.

A mental image is an excellent way to follow along. Apart from visuals, you can experience impressions, hear something audible in your mind, or be cleverly steered from one thought to another to help you understand the idea more effectively. It's simply a matter of being receptive and allowing for this fluidity.

If you are conducting extensive research on a significant topic, you may open the third eye area and request guidance in the following manner;

Who is familiar with this subject?

Who can quickly respond to my questions?

To whom do I need to speak?" "

Where can I locate him or her at this time or in a short period?

If you're on the internet, ask yourself, "What search term or expression would get me my response immediately?"

Then, when you receive impressions, act immediately and place your confidence in the details. When you have confidence, it will manifest more easily. When you perform a therapeutic function, such as administering Reiki to another, you can listen in and get precise details about the person you are operating. You will learn about their emotional and physical well-being, spiritual quest, actions, and long-buried emotional roots.

When you function in a healing capacity, many factors come into play. Your paws and heart and third eye are conduits; many practitioners experience impressions from the chakras and aura fields of the body.

Also, healing guides, angels, and the person's totem or spirit guides are assisting you. You must develop the ability to work with as many elements as you feel comfortable with and separate multiple elements simultaneously. When you begin working in earnest, you will become very familiar with different elements.

You can use both masters the third eye and function in profound spiritual relation. You must keep an eye on the balance. Not all is mastered in a single sitting. Not all data is processed concurrently. If your goal is clear and you want clarification, all will become clear. Practice, take your time, believe in yourself, and allow your light to shine.

How to Improve The Skills

Not everyone has worked actively to develop third-eye wisdom or understanding. Many people are terrified of their ability to get intelligence or knowledge that seems to come from nowhere. Others are unconcerned with where it comes from and simply access it.

Now, when you practice with the third eye for extended periods, you improve the capacity to reach psychic sources, but it can also exhaust you if you do not maintain a healthy balance. I feel as if it's a trap that can't be left open all the time.

Close the door and take a break. When you're ready to close the area, place your hand on your forehead and move it from top to bottom as if you're closing a large gate or a drawbridge door.

Then tell yourself, "I'm going to shut down now." Like a psychic wash, inhale deeply into that place. With breath, you mentally bathe the area in light. Occasionally, you might fool yourself into believing that you turn off a light bulb by pulling an old-fashioned cord. The region becomes pitch black. Just like the light bulb, you can easily turn it back on.

Develop as much sensitivity as possible to slight shifts in energy and ask yourself if they are coming from you or anyone else. Also, send out a feeler to determine if this is true or false. Inquire about the information that is being sent.

"How am I to use this?"

"Is this about whom?"

"How do you want me to use this knowledge?"

When you are working actively with your third eye, guide your attention to a point on the bridge or tip of your nose. Close your eyes halfway to allow for an unobstructed view into the psychic world through the third eye and allow this region to open completely.

Consider the drawbridge door gradually rising and opening. The column of light then expands outward into the world, being as long or as short as necessary.

You may have the impression that the light is only coming from the front of your forehead. Alternatively, you may feel more like an egg with a large crack running around the circumference and many small cracks on the top and back.

The light found inside will radiate out simultaneously from all the cracks on the front, back, top, and sides, allowing you to see all around you. Although the majority originates in the front or third eye region, it is not limited to that.

After becoming aware of the energetic changes, you can begin directing your channel. You may reflect on a particular topic or individual and pose questions. Try to breathe through each question as you ask it. Allow some time between each query to allow the details to register.

You might also think about someone or something and feel what immediate and first thoughts come to mind. Carry out this action without judgment. Believe in yourself and the ability to receive the correct answer.

You might ask, "What am I missing here?" or "What is the critical component?" Enable an open flow to guide you - "Guide me to the individual or community most capable of assisting me." Then anticipate being guided and continue as if you are already on your way.

Creative Projects Using the Third Eye

If you are a novelist, your third eye experience will come in handy frequently. Open your mind deliberately before you begin writing and, if you're working on a subject you're unfamiliar with, quietly ask yourself, "What do you want me to say about this?" Sometimes, you'll become deeply linked, but your vision will become hazy.

Continue looking at the page until the words begin to appear on it. The experience can give the impression that the page is extremely deep and you are peering into the very depths of this three-dimensional space.

The words will come into focus very soon, and you will see the sentence beginning to form on the screen. Often, you are unaware of what you have written and it sounds very insightful when reading back. Alternatively, you may use the same strategy to generate story or script ideas. The concept and the characters begin to take shape.

If you share my experience, you can begin to hear the characters conversing and simply transcribe what you hear. At times, the dialogue begins in your mind and you have no idea where it is going, what context the dialogue is being spoken in or where the characters are located. Simply follow along before you're able to keep up with the action.

Sometimes, a character will visit you. You may catch yourself conversing with him or her or watching them in different circumstances, such as having lunch, attending a friend's wedding, investigating something, receiving a payment, plotting a murder or escaping, or when they are caught in an unusual circumstance and how they respond spontaneously.

Another way to use the third eye perspective is to do something artistic, such as drawing. If this applies to you, consider the concept and begin defocusing your eyes until your third eye opens, at which point you can invite the painter in.

For me, whoever assisted me possessed an infinite knowledge of perspective, landscapes, color detail, and shadowing and demonstrated to me an exact location where he or she had been but more importantly, moved the brush in the right way to complete the sketch. When you are conscious and employ third eye awareness in this manner, you can complete masterful tasks in a reasonably short period.

What Is the Third Eye's Primary Focus?

In mindfulness practice, it is said that we have a third eye referred to as our "Mind's Eye." How we choose to focus this enlightened eye has a significant impact on our inner feelings and the decisions we create on how we show up in our everyday lives.

For the sake of this segment, let us assume that we have two options for focusing on this illustrious third eye. Also, let us consider the impact of these choices on our interpersonal relationships. The first three are universal primary needs that must be met at a level eight (on a one to ten scale) 80% of the time to have a caring, linked, and harmonious relationship.

Security, assurance, and confidence are the first three requirements. You can calculate your score for these requirements by responding to the following query. If that is the case, the next question is whether you have shared your definition or, as I like to call it, what constitutes deposits for each of your three needed banks with your partner.

If you are unaware of what you require and/or have not shared this information with your partner, how can he or she make deposits to ensure that your account is brimming with funds?

So, how does all of this relate to the third eye?

If our Minds Eye is guided inward, we are in an "I" centric frame of reference. When this occurs, we are more concerned with ourselves than with others. We are more concerned with what we receive than with what we offer. We are more concerned with jealousy than with appreciation. We are more concerned with how the world treats us than with what we do with the world.

When our Mind's Eye is directed inward, it is entirely based on "ME." Rather than being attuned to others' thoughts and emotions, we would ignore them. Instead of finding understanding and feeling empathy, we will experience increased anxiety and irritation with others and life circumstances. From an "I" centric Mind's Eye, we will respond to life's flow in ways that numb and separate us rather than nurturing and connecting.

Through focusing our Mind's Eye on the "I" rather than the "WE," we can manifest stories in which we relinquish our strength, succumb to the winds of change, and end up generating inner suffrage. This will force us to withdraw from the banks of stability, certainty, and confidence of our partners.

Suppose you're ready to develop and encouraged to build a partnership in which each partner's primary needs for protection, certainty, and confidence are met at level 8 at least 80% of the time, keep your third eye open, and when we develop the habit of using the Mind's Eye's strength in an "I" centric manner. In that case, we will fail in our relationship with ourselves and with our spouse.

Unleash Your Psychic Abilities by Unlocking Your Third Eye

A psychic can use his or her other intuitive abilities for personal growth and improve the circumstances in which they find themselves. You must first improve your psychic abilities before you can open your third eye and unleash your abilities. Your mind will always be flooded with images and ideas.

Belief is the first step toward effectively unleashing your psychic instincts. The reality is that some individuals are born with superior intuition, just as some individuals are born with superior physical abilities.

But, if a person believes they cannot have a specific ability simply because they were not born with it, they will not improve it. Once you recognize that you are a human with infinite potential, you will understand that you can develop any ability if you want it.

Only when you accept that the more you trust your feelings and instincts, the more they work for you will you unleash your psychic abilities. Many who trust their gut instincts always see their dreams come true. Those with subtle perceptions and self-doubt often struggle in their endeavors. You should keep in mind that intuition functions best on first impressions.

The second reality about releasing your inner awareness is that you will have immediate perceptive information about something that comes from your subconscious mind within the first few moments of experiencing it before your conscious mind takes over your emotions. You will develop your psychic abilities by focusing your mind and attitude on the initial impressions you have about a situation.

While psychic abilities are possible inside us, many instruments can activate one's natural abilities. There are some of these, including astrology, psychometry, palmistry, and oracles.

Psychometry is a technique that utilizes an instrument to detect the energy of the individual being read. This instrument or object is personal to the owner and a psychic can predict the owner's future.

Palmistry is an ancient method of releasing one's inner energies. It is an ancient art form that incorporates many intuitive elements. It interprets the lines on the hand and makes decisions based on the psychic elements incorporated into the interpretation.

Astrology is a form of psychic reading that uses special Zodiac signs that contain records of many ancient events that correspond to the modern scheme of things. Astrology is a psychic instrument that examines past life regressions; it is believed that everyone spends some time in a previous life before entering the present one.

You can activate your psychic abilities on your own by paying attention to your dreams and intuition. While some dreams are merely recitations of the day's events, others may foreshadow future events and dreams that often lack significance for the dreamer but reflect something.

Keep a journal of your dreams and pay close attention to what occurs many days later. Link real-life events and dream symbolism. Pay attention to your instincts in the small stuff and you might be surprised to discover a link between your dreams and events occurring in reality.

Third Eye Development

To stimulate the third eye and experience higher dimensions, the pineal gland and pituitary body must vibrate in lockstep, which can be accomplished through meditation and relaxation. When a proper relationship between personality, which operates through the pituitary body and soul, a magnetic field is generated.

The visualization exercise is the first step toward focusing the energies within your inner system in the direction of activating the third eye. By concentrating the mind on the midpoint between the pineal gland and the pituitary body, the magnetic field is produced around the pineal gland. The imaginative imagination visualizes something and the mind's thinking energy gives this form life and direction.

Third, eye creation, imagination, and visualization are critical components of many techniques for dissociating from the physical body. Third-eye intuition is also possible.

The astral plane's knowledge and memory are not recorded in a fully awakened consciousness until the intuition becomes sufficiently powerful. Flashes of insight become more consistent as the third eye becomes more stimulated through practice.

After shutting their eyes, everyone sees images or forms, but most do not pay attention to them because they are not programmed. Your higher self, your spirit guides, or other spirit friends can send you photos. These images can take some time to grasp, but there is no rush.

Many indigenous rituals and magical practices refer to the ability to see or be conscious of higher-level energy fields. Abstract perception is significantly more subjective than mundane consciousness, which is primarily concerned with self-identification. This vision refers to the third eye's vision.

The third eye is an organ of the light body, also known as the etheric body or energy body. The third eye, when opened, provides access to the soul's layers or measurements. The spirit, in my opinion, is the light being's memories. These memories include the past, current, and future aspects of what some people refer to as time.

The third eye serves as a portal or gateway to space's multidimensionality, represented as either space or time. Travel is possible by passing through a doorway to another world.

Many individuals have had a degree of experience with this through hallucinations and visions. Individuals with a tuned third eye have increased freedom of choice and transparency.

Equivalent to cleaning the lenses of a camera, tuning the third eye is a similar process. This clears the third eye of obstructions and debris leftovers from past, current, future, and life traumas. Once triggered, the third eye serves as a direct conduit for perceptual contact between the light and physical bodies.

Historically, people who are committed to planetary harmony have used the third eye. Your spirit guide oversees the entire process. The third eye's extreme sensitivity is easily influenced by moods, food, drink, and narcotics. Individuals with a perpetually open third eye have a propensity for excessive stimulation.

These individuals may experience distress from noise sources such as television or radio and other electromagnetic equipment; in these instances, the third eye is jammed open due to excessive activity-sensorial overload. This puts undue strain on the body and skews the soul's communication system.

If you've established contact with your third eye, you'll feel as though you're floating in an ocean of electricity. This sense is developed through different activities found in various cultures, including meditation, relaxation, and sport.

It is not an action that generates the sense of the third eye; rather, it is the third eye that generates a sense of equilibrium, concentration, attention, cohesion, and flows in your success. The third eye is in control of the light body's independence of intention. Due to this, the third eye exerts control over one's individuality and imagination.

The Third Eye serves as the civilization's portal to the future. As a civilization, we will have to recognize our light bodies as the aspect of the soul in charge of planet maintenance.

Here is an exercise that you will wish to attempt.

Sit calmly and empty the mind of distractions and clutter. Take a few slow deep breaths and begin focusing on the mental screen.

The appearance of colors should begin. Continue to observe the colors and take a long, deep breath. The colors will now combine to form an object that you may or may not know.

If you cannot see anything, it is possible that you are not comfortable or anxious. If this occurs, simply return later in the day and attempt again.

CHAPTER 2: CLEARING OUT ENERGY FIELDS

Regularly clearing your energy field has a noticeable effect on your healing work and everyday life. Negative energy, aura tangles, and cords connecting you to others all become a drain on your energy flow.

When doing healing work, your relationship with others becomes more intense, making you more vulnerable to negative energies. You must develop proficiency in clearing your energy of any debris you can pick up if you want to practice healing. This section discusses some fundamental cleaning techniques for maintaining a balanced energy field.

Auric Purification

Visualize, feel, or otherwise perceive an egg-shaped energy field surrounding your body, composed of strands of flowing energy radiating outward from the center of your being to approximately. 5 to 1 meter in length. It resembles a soft flowing energy rug.

Consider taking a shower (this is particularly effective if you are already in the shower!)

Instead of water, the liquid is sparkling white light that penetrates deeply into your energy field, dissolving negative energy, untangling knots, and soothing away wrinkles. You can also use fictitious white light shampoo and conditioner to spruce up your energy field before covering yourself and returning to your normal life.

Corsets

Whenever you engage with someone on a deep level - whether you support them, have a friendship with them, or perform healing on them - a cord is formed between you two depending on the type of relationship (or aspect of relationship) you have

These cords may be beneficial in a stable, caring relationship; In an unhealthy relationship or a temporary relationship (or part of a relationship) such as healing work, the cords become exhausting, to the point of causing illness if not severed.

Cord-cutting is a multi-tiered process. The most basic level is for new cords, for relationships that were brief or relatively unimportant, and/or for cords that you are no longer attached to.

Consider cords emerging from the body and connecting to those on the other side. They may be very thin, such as optic wire, or much thicker. Invoke

Archangel Michael and implore him to 'please sever any cords wasting my energy right now!'

The firm attitude is not intended to be disrespectful; rather, it suggests the unity of purpose. Recognize that you have the choice of not having these cords attached to you and that you have the right and ability to have them fully removed.

Cords from deeper or more complex relationships can require you to pay more attention to detail and demonstrate a greater degree of commitment. You will need to concentrate on the individual cord, identify the person to whom it is attached and make a direct promise to Archangel Michael that you no longer want this link with this person (this does not mean that you must completely cut ties with the person but you can if you wish).

By concentrating on the cord and its connection to you and visualizing the person on the other end of the cord (it can feel as though they are right in front of you at this point), communicate to Archangel Michael that you are ready to cut the cord and release this person.

Inhale deeply, and then quickly exhale, squeezing the air out of your lungs by leaning over if possible as Archangel Michael cuts the rope with his sword. Stop, check and double-check that the cord is fully severed; it normally disconnects the first time, but with deeper commitments, the procedure can need to be repeated many times.

All of this work is necessary and necessary. It is limited to simpler layers of congested and dark energy; it cannot deal with Dark Consciousness or intrusion. To deal with this more subtle and difficult-to-locate part of energy work, you will need specialized training in energy work.

Techniques For Clearing Others' Emotions And Thoughts

Bear in mind that thoughts are objects and that what you think about expands. When you prepare and envision the following tools, keep in mind that you influence your energy and experience in real-time.

1) Inviting your Personal Energy Field to join you is the first step.

Although you may not have expanded your field knowingly, you may consciously retract it. Since you are in control of your being, you can order your field to contract as tightly as you wish, all the way to the edge of your body if you are in direct contact with others. This can require some practice to perfect and maintain, but you can improve your skills over time.

2) Topography

As with electrical devices, the human body can be stabilized by consciously connecting its energy to the earth. While it is possible to ground by visualizing roots arising from your feet, I believe that grounding from the first chakra at the base of the spine into the earth's heart, using the image of a tunnel, is more potent.

3) Elimination

Make the intention to release any energy that is no longer beneficial to you or serves your highest good; you can send it directly down your Grounding Tube for recycling and transmutation! This can take as little as a few moments or as many as twenty minutes or more, depending on how often you take out the garbage!

4) Rose

A rose is an excellent tool for this since it has the highest frequency on the planet; many people use it for energy clearing, thereby inspiring it, and it has a built-in grounding line in the long stem!

Each of these energy alchemy strategies has had a profound impact on my life and I employ them daily; I also teach them in greater depth during our Quantum Creating retreats. For instance, I was unaware of the extent to which I felt my own emotions and those of others, especially those close to me.

My husband and I were rapidly escalating an argument one night and the temperature was 9. Fortunately, I had recently learned how to create separations using the Rose method, and unbeknownst to him, I "inserted" a rose between us on the couch and started clearing. Instantly, I felt as if the bulk of the uproar was directed against his side of the rose and I was now down to a.

A 5-Step Procedure for Eliminating Emotional Undercurrents in Your Energy Field

Water teaches you in different ways, as varied as the types she takes — seas, rivers, lakes, streams, rain, ice, drinking water, bathing water, hot water hail, snow sleet. Water teaches you in the realm of feelings and emotions, which can vary from frozen, cold, steamy, hot, smooth, soft, calm to rough as a day out at sea.

Your emotions provide critical guidance and teachings about your life and business and everyone has a different level of comfort with feeling and working with them. Few people are taught how to honor and work with their emotions as children, even though emotional maturity is a necessary component of full effectiveness. Water teaches you to cultivate greater levels of emotional savvies.

But what if there is an undercurrent in your watery emotional realm, something that threatens to pull you down, hold you small, or quell your dreams?

What if you are filled with self-doubt or relinquish your power?

An emotional undercurrent is something that is often held due to childhood; it is something that is beneath the surface that was usually infused into your inner water (or emotional realm) before you were even aware of the existence of emotions and undercurrents;

you felt the emotions but had no conscious knowledge of them.

A common undercurrent is an insecurity. Sometimes, this is a form of childhood programming in which the child is made to feel insecure for parents or teachers to exert further control over the child.

Religious training may often result in this type of "power over." The resulting insecurity the child feels becomes infused with emotional water without the child's conscious consent.

What clears an emotional undercurrent is a reality. Often, old feelings draw experiences into your life rather than pure, clean water saturated with truth. Your mind is saying, "I want to build this, this and this," but something is impeding you.

The Five Steps To Clearing Your Emotional Undercurrents Are As Follows:

1. Recognize and accept the underlying current. Inquire as to what undercurrent is driving you at the moment. How do you feel about the work you're doing?

Consider the undercurrent and give it a tag. If it's insecurity, state explicitly, "Wow, okay, I can feel that as insecurity." If it's envy, state explicitly, "Wow, okay, I can feel that as jealousy." In each case, state, "Wow, I can feel that as well" (fill in the blank).

2. Recognize the unmet emotional needs that the

undercurrent is bringing to you. Sometimes, the unmet emotional need is for approval and praise. Even as you get older, you can find yourself going through your life and business with a strong desire for a parent or another person to approve of you because it makes you feel good. That is an unmet need.

3. Consider the impact that each unmet need has had on your life and business. For example, whether it's insecurity, it might have caused you to stop doing something in response to criticism or when you didn't receive enough approval or praise. Inwardly, you lacked the emotional clarity to continue following your inner guidance when you weren't receiving what you expected externally.

4. After examining the impact and influence, it's time to clear any unmet needs. To do so, begin by making a clear statement. For example, suppose you're clearing insecurity or the unmet need for approval, praise, and recognition. Using the power of intention, simply say, "I clear any unmet need for approval, praise or recognition." Breathe deeply and repeat.

5. Infuse a new message into your inner water. Water reacts to messages and emotions injected into it; it is an aspect that you can imprint. This is a very effective thing to do, but it must be done intentionally.

To infuse a new message into your inner water, use prayer or affirmation-type sentences. For example, you may say, "You're doing an excellent job." "I approve, recognize, and compliment myself."

Or "I love myself." I appreciate what I'm doing." "I infuse grace and ease; I let go of the need to be perfect and allow myself to create actively." There are endless possibilities for creation, but you must infuse your inner Water with a message that makes you feel expansive and uplifted.

As an adult, you are responsible for the treatment of your inner Water. Even if your inner Water contains residual energy from your childhood, once you learn how to recognize and clear what has been infused as an undercurrent, you will no longer be forced to work with emotions that hold you back. Using the five steps outlined above, keep your inner Water — your emotional domain — crystal clear and full of reality.

CHAPTER 3:
ENCOURAGING THOUGHTS

If you see a surfer ride a wave, you'll find that the wave gradually turns into a large swell, which surges into a larger wave, bringing the surfer to the shore.

Thoughts pass through the landscape of your mind like ocean waves; new ones join your stream of consciousness every second, which means that thoughts are transient unless you focus your attention on a single one.

We exist in the emotions associated with our feelings, not in the external circumstances that affect them; external circumstances do not impose on your thinking but can evoke an emotional response if the stimulus is sufficiently intense. A thought can evoke a negative emotion on some days, while it may be insignificant on others.

How did this happen?

Apart from that day, what has changed?

At those times, we respond to our surroundings for unexplained reasons, such as being tired, moody, or hungry. At that point, we are more ruled by our thoughts.

Your mind is incapable of distinguishing between positive and negative thoughts. It does not record them in this way - but you, the observer, do. When we mark feelings, we elevate them above others, allowing them to take up space in our minds.

To be perfectly plain, you are not your feelings.

You are not your feelings, as they appear and vanish from your consciousness, with none remaining permanent. They can be replicated many times, but they are never irreversible. To suggest that you are

what you think is deceptive, to the extent that you might have a positive thought one minute and a negative thought the next. If the distinction defines you, who are you according to this narrative?

If we live in the emotions associated with our thoughts and have anxious thoughts, this does not mean we are anxious people. This indicates that you encountered a feeling that induced fear in your body.

You might have an enlightening thought the next moment that cancels out the previous one. Of course, there are exceptions determined by a psychiatric diagnosis made by a licensed mental health professional.

The key to overcoming unwanted thoughts is to be mindful of them, not to eject them from your mind.

Thoughts pass through your mind between 50,000 and 70,000 per day. Thoughts pass through your mind on a moment-by-moment basis, just like a live television broadcast.

How Do We Counteract The Detrimental Consequences Of Thoughts That Reach Our Consciousness?

By being aware of disempowering feelings, you bring them to the forefront of the mind and bring them into the realm of consciousness rather than the realm of the unconscious.

Unconscious thoughts are a common part of our mental state, similar to how a pop-up window advertising a product or service will confuse you when watching a television show on a computer.

The objective is to watch the film but the distraction distracts you. Unconscious thoughts have a similar effect; they come out of nowhere and lead us into dangerous territory if we are not careful.

"The pain you produce now is often a manifestation of non-acceptance, some manifestation of unintentional opposition to what is. On a mental level, resistance takes the form of adjudication. It is some kind of negativity on an emotional level.

Your level of resistance determines the severity of the pain to the present moment, determined by your degree of identification with your mind. The trick is to become aware of our unconscious thoughts without eliciting negative emotions or introducing a narrative. We do this by witnessing them with equanimity rather than responding with negative emotions or behavior.

To begin riding the wave of positive thinking, take note of the sensations that arise in your body. Take note of your emotional reaction without being emotionally involved in it. According to Eckhart Tolle, "Emotions emerge at the point where the mind and body collide. It is the body's response to your mind - or, as some may suggest, a physical manifestation of your mind."

Empowering thoughts have an enlightening quality, as they demonstrate peace and equilibrium. Uncomfortable sensations are the body's way of communicating that your thoughts are out of balance.

In this context, the body serves as a feedback instrument that informs you of your thoughts. You are not required to be aware of every thought. By being conscious of how your thoughts produce positive or negative feelings, you can select more healthy thoughts.

When an inspirational thought occurs, bring your awareness to your body and note your emotional reaction.

Is it in your chest, neck, or another part of your body?

What does it feel like?

Is it a radiating tingling feeling or does it spread to other areas?

Meditation is beneficial when you are alone with your thoughts in a peaceful environment. Even five minutes of silence lets you become familiar with your emotions, rather than allowing them to move through your mind unnoticed.

To ride the wave of positive thought, take note of the emotions they elicit when focusing your attention on them. As you observe your emotions, your consciousness diminishes their power. Through practice, you can develop longer streams of optimistic thoughts as you become accustomed to their ebb and flow.

How to Quiet That Inner Negative Voice

Therefore, one would assume that a large number of people are now completely reaping the rewards of positive thinking, correct? Not.

To be sure, many people use positive thinking to their advantage, but unfortunately, not nearly as many people who might profit do so.

Why is this the case?

There are different reasons why someone does not benefit completely from positive thinking. Still, one of the primary issues is difficulty developing and sustaining the habit of thinking positive thoughts.

You may have had this experience yourself; you set out to practice positive thinking and it may go well for a day or even a week, but then you find yourself doing it less and less often until the exercise is completely forgotten.

Does that ring a bell?

If this is the case, do not be too harsh on yourself; you are not alone. Therefore, why does this occur, and more importantly, what can we do to resolve this issue and develop the habit of thinking positive thoughts?

Why Is It So Difficult to Have Positive Thoughts?

Positive thinking is more difficult for some people than others. There are often powerful unconscious thoughts that are very pessimistic for those who struggle to maintain a positive outlook on life, sabotaging our attempts to think positively.

It can be extremely difficult to maintain a positive attitude if the little voice in your head is constantly contradicting your positive thoughts and replacing them with negative ones! This is particularly true when we are unaware of our negative thoughts.

The negative inner voice has an inherent advantage; it has existed for a long period. The inner voice is composed of links between brain cells that have been reinforced over time and, most likely, by feedback indicating that they have aided you.

"You aided me, huh!?" Yes, it is irrational, but if one thinks negatively, such as "If the statement "I can't do that; I'll just stay home" or "I'll just embarrass myself" is accompanied by a decrease in anxiety. This effectively communicates the message "that thought aided me." I'm doing much better now."

Yes, it aided you in the short term, but it is no longer assisting you at all.

How Can I Quiet My Inner Negative Voice?

Since the Inner Voice is such a formidable enemy, you must use the appropriate technique to defeat it effectively. The first step is to keep your optimistic affirmations subtle and unobtrusive.

For instance, if I am self-conscious about my appearance, I can avoid powerfully positive statements such as "I am stunning" or "I am a beautiful girl." These are so at odds with my inner voice's thoughts that it will become even more adamant in its attempts to be understood. As a result, it will almost certainly be difficult for you to believe those optimistic thoughts are valid.

Positive thinking that you do not believe to be true would do you no good. Rather than that, we should begin with something optimistic that does not directly contradict our negative inner voice.

Because, I might say, "I am not that bad-looking." That does act as a counterbalance to negative thinking, but in a far more subtle way. Psychologists refer to these types of constructive thinking as 'balancing thoughts' at times.

These more subtle balancing thoughts are less upsetting to your inner voice and generate significantly less resistance. They are more easily believed and due to this, they appear to last longer. You are on your way to finally silencing the negative inner voice with a series of optimistic balancing thoughts!

The Critical Role of Positive Thoughts in Your Mind

It cannot be overstated how important it is to fill your mind with positive thoughts. Positive and negative thoughts work similarly to traffic signals. Positive thoughts imply progress, while negative ones are often viewed as stop signs. Positive thoughts allow progress, while negative thoughts obstruct progress. Without constructive thinking, plans grind to a halt.

The trick is to see negative thoughts as detour signs rather than stop signs. They warn of hazards, which is very positive. They allow maneuvering around impediments. This is how to turn negative emotions into constructive ones. Avoid being too dogmatic in your thoughts. To a salesperson, the term "no" means "maybe," and "maybe" means "yes." Positivity will still find a way.

It all depends on your perspective. Two sales representatives were sent to Africa to sell shoes. One sent a telegram to his company canceling the order, claiming that no one wears shoes in this country. The other doubled his order, believing it to be limitless.

There is often an alternate viewpoint. Examine all possible angles and you're likely to come across one that has promise. Filling your mind with good thoughts will help you identify the most advantageous angle.

Positive thoughts breed hope, whereas negative ones breed pessimism. Positive thoughts are fueled by passion, while a lack of excitement fuels negative ones. The distinction is comparable to that of day and night.

This demonstrates the critical nature of surrounding yourself with optimistic thoughts. Without hope and zeal, you will perish. Your only chance is to summon some optimistic thinking.

There are times when the risk of failure is so high that it is prudent not to continue. In this instance, your negative thoughts benefit you. They enable you to change your course and avoid potential pitfalls. Consider your negative energy as a friend, not an adversary. When you heed their warnings, your good thoughts will help you avoid danger.

The trick is to prevent your negative energy from running amok. It is not attempting to deter you from proceeding; rather, it demonstrates what not to do. From there, the optimistic side will take over and lead you to victory.

Similarly, do not allow your optimistic energy to carry you forward without regard for the risk. Consider the positive and negative aspects as a check and balance system. Success is analogous to driving a vehicle. If you make an abrupt left or right turn, you risk causing a crash. You must know when to proceed and when to halt.

You cannot become too ecstatic about your positive energy, nor can you panic when you experience negative thoughts. This demonstrates the critical nature of effectively controlling your emotions to advance to a good career.

How to Maintain Positive Thoughts

Have you ever heard the adage that it becomes a habit if you do something consistently for twenty or thirty days?

To be sure, there is a great deal of reality in that.

Thus, the true secret to sustaining such optimistic thoughts over time is to stick with them for the first three to four weeks. By beginning with balancing thoughts that do not elicit excessive opposition from your inner ear, you have already gained a significant advantage.

To stack the odds in your favor, you should set an external reminder to review and refresh your balancing thoughts regularly. This can be accomplished with a few basic cards carried in your wallet.

On the cards, jot down the constructive balancing thoughts (it's also fun to decorate them!) and peruse them during the day. If you want a more high-tech solution, various applications are available for smartphones that remind you to review the information you enter into them regularly.

How Much Do I Remind Myself of My Positive Thoughts?

Consider going through the thoughts as you awaken before you go to bed and at least three to four other times during the day. You can adjust this to suit your schedule but do not go below four times a day (including when you wake up and when you go to bed).

Do I simply read the thoughts or am I to take action?

While you read the thoughts, you want to ensure that the message they contain is felt to the fullest extent possible.

It's a good idea to develop the habit of reading through optimistic thoughts if you have some free time. When practicing positive thinking, it's best to stop being rushed, distracted or concerned about someone looking over your shoulder.

When you have a moment to yourself and will not be interrupted, begin by relaxing and breathing normally. There is no need to engage in a lengthy relaxation routine; we just want to create a psychological buffer between ourselves and our daily stresses and remain positive.

Then, one by one, read through each thought. As you read through each thought, keep in mind that it is directed at you. Sensitize yourself to the reality of what you are reading as you process each thought, smile, and encourage yourself to experience some joy and peace.

What Comes Next?

After a few days to a week of practicing your optimistic thinking, you will likely begin to look forward to each session. You will develop an appreciation for the enjoyable feelings and emotions associated with your optimistic thoughts. If you meditate, you can also try going through your thoughts while in a deep state of relaxation.

When you are fully at ease with your optimistic thoughts and encounter no opposition or disbelief in response to them, you are ready to move on to more strong positive thinking.

Daily Positive Thoughts

Regular positive thinking is critical; keeping a positive outlook during the day is difficult, even if you come from a default pessimistic mindset. Often you'll wake up in an extremely optimistic mood and other times not so much; the best way to ensure that you remain positive is to exercise self-control and indulge in positive thinking.

So, how do I go about doing this?

I used Smash Mouth's "All-Star" as my alarm clock; it might sound cheesy, but it woke me up on a positive note. Later on, I developed an aversion to it, as we do to all of my alarm clock sounds, don't we?

That was not far from the correct way to go about it; begin each day with positive thoughts. The song encapsulates what positivity is, essentially, reckless self-promotion and inspiration.

Therefore, I reasoned, why not tell myself the things that inspire me? That is, most of the time, we continually tell ourselves negative things.

Why not exert some influence over this and, rather than flooding our minds with negativity, flood them with positivity?

This is how the idea for my list of affirmations came about; I read about it on a few websites and, to be frank, thought it was a little stupid and cheesy but still made sense. If you tell yourself something regularly, you will eventually believe it; people always do this with negative thoughts, as I previously said, and it works. Therefore, let us use it positively!

This works by having you repeat meaningful lines and feelings to yourself. They do not have to be true; for instance, repeating the phrase "I am sure" may be considered one and. Even if you do not consider yourself optimistic, it is inspiring and will assist you in developing that belief.

You should focus on developing your list; this is particularly beneficial in the early stages of improving your social aspect. It enables you to begin making mental changes.

I'll share mine with you, my very own daily positive thoughts list, to assist you in creating your own:

I am the guy who converses with others.

I exude a strong sense of self-assurance and a truly uncommon sense of humor.

I exude an air of warmth around me and people enjoy conversing with me.

I command authority and regard.

I am a cool person.

I have a large social circle, good acquaintances, and am constantly involved in social events.

Beautiful women surround me in my social circles and most of them are interested in me.

I do seem to be surrounded by beautiful females.

I have the most interesting and amusing stories to tell; I am an excellent storyteller.

Every day, the best and funniest things happen to me.

I lead an active social life and am involved in all the cool stuff going on.

Those are motivational thoughts because they helped me visualize who I desired to be; even though I no longer use this "affirmation list," those were the constant optimistic thoughts that stayed with me. I resurrected the list from my old archives and I'm just now realizing how many of those good thoughts have become true!

As I previously said, it is highly beneficial in the early stages of social and confidence growth, so give it a try; constructive propaganda for your mind. Create your list of affirmations and jot them down! For a while, read them intermittently during the day to bring positivity to your life!

CHAPTER 4:
ENERGY MEDITATION

Energy meditation is a technique for channeling the universe's energies into your own body for attunement and wellness. There are various types of energy, including Reiki and Mahatma. Meditation is an ancient practice that is said to assist in relieving stress and anxiety, promoting a sense of peace, and even promoting longevity.

According to energy meditation principles, people have "auras" surrounding them with energy centers referred to as "chakras." Some individuals are said to be able to see chakras. Also, there are methods for photographing them. Each energy has a unique vibration and meditating enables one to become more aware of their own.

Since chakra energies are at various stages, it takes time and effort to progress to them, but they can broaden spiritual knowledge and consciousness. All in our environment is made up of energy. Inner harmony is achieved by meditating on this. Anyone can meditate in the comfort of their own homes. All that is needed is a quiet room and some free time.

The meditator then concentrates on a mantra, a spoken word, an object, an image, or something else they wish to focus on. It needs preparation and a great deal of patience. Although sitting quietly for twenty minutes is difficult, with practice, it is possible. The meditator emerges from the meditation satisfied, rejuvenated, and renewed.

Spreading positive and kind thoughts around the universe is another part of energy meditation. When we meditate on these topics, we gain a clearer understanding of the larger picture and where we need to be in our lives, and the steps necessary to get there.

Meditation can assist in relaxing and relieving stresses, fears, and pressures and assisting in relieving health issues so that the meditator does not become stressed by them. Meditation methods may function as a driving force, assisting people in finding balance in their life.

Suppose you've been practicing energy meditation for a while or are new to it, whether it's qigong, Core Energy meditation, pranayama, kundalini, or another system. In that case, I believe you'll find the following eight tips beneficial to your development. Many of these tips also refer to other types of meditation practices.

Meditation is the practice of concentrating your attention on a single item or behavior for an extended period. Energy meditation entails visualizing and sensing your vital energy, prana or "qi" ("chee") as your focal point.

The energy centers and pathways that run through your body are excellent for meditation because they provide an active route for your mind to follow. It's fascinating and it generally feels great—even more so after you've honed your skills.

Energy therapy anchors you to the present moment in your body, which is an important way to "de-stress." Also, it has many health benefits, including activation of your natural calming reflex, better posture, stress release, increased circulation, deeper breathing, more coherent brain, and heart function, and an improved immune response. Energy meditation promotes a sense of well-being, optimism, and vitality.

Most significantly, it establishes a link between you and the heart of "who you are" and "what you came here to do." It establishes a connection between you and your intuitive guidance, deeper meaning, and feelings of oneness with life.

We focus on three main energy centers or dantians ("Dahn-tee-ens") in your body in the Chinese method of qigong and Core Energy:

1. Your lower dantian or Body Center, located in your lower abdomen, is associated with your primal life force and physical vitality.

2. Your middle dantian or Heart Core, located in the center of your chest, is associated with refined emotions and interpersonal attributes such as respect, gratitude, confidence, compassion, and affection.

3. The upper dantian or Mind Core, located in the center of your brain, is associated with your mental faculties of insight, creativity, intuition, and focus and your ability to analyze your perceptions peacefully and without being overwhelmed by them.

When you first begin practicing imagining and sensing your energy centers, you will not have anything to imagine or experience. It can be difficult to maintain an emphasis on them in your practice. Also, it is normal to feel one of them but not the others or to feel two of them but not the other.

What you perceive is determined by your inherent ability for visualization and kinesthetic sensing, the degree to which your energy centers are activated, and how much you have practiced sensing within your body.

It is appropriate to be at any level of capacity to imagine and feel inside your body. Regardless of your current skills, you will benefit from adding yourself to the practice. With continued practice, you will increasingly develop the ability to experience, sense, collect, circulate, refine, and still your inner life force.

As your skills develop, you will find improvements in your ability to discern inner direction, make wise decisions, be present and carry out your best intentions. You will develop a sense of belonging, fitness, and optimism in your body, heart, mind, and spirit.

You will establish a consistent personal energetic vibration that is solid, optimistic, simple, and coherent, or what I like to refer to as a "Core Energy State." Here are eight suggestions to keep you moving forward.

Effective Energy Meditation Techniques:

To begin, practice daily. If you practice only when you believe you need it, keep in mind that there is far more to the practice than just using it to relax and re-center yourself when you become "stressed out" (though this is certainly important).

If you practice daily, you will find that you are more capable of processing the experiences and tensions of the previous 24 hours, allowing you to approach life with a much clearer, calm, hopeful, and concentrated perspective.

You can also note a difference if you skip even a single day of practice, as unresolved emotions begin to cloud your vision and affect your mood. It's normal to experience letting go of "old things" that may bubble up into your consciousness during your first few years of practice. The more of these repressed tensions you release, the more openly you can live in the present.

To help you maintain a routine, I recommend that you pick a period that seems very appropriate to you, maybe 15-20 minutes, and schedule it at the same time each day (for example, first thing in the morning). Though waking up earlier can be difficult at first, you're likely to develop an appetite for waking up and entering a "Core Energy State."

The primary reason for regular practice is that you can immediately begin your practice and expand on what you did the previous day each time you sit down. You'll remain in sync with it. If you practice infrequently or sporadically, you will essentially "always be starting over."

2. If you've been training regularly for some time, you might want to consider growing your practice time. While 15-20 minutes daily is ideal, you may find that meditating for longer periods strengthens and deepens the benefits. The more you meditate, the deeper, smoother, and quieter the states become.

It's common for the first 10-15 minutes of practice to be filled with mind chatter, which gradually subsides as time passes. If you sit for at least 30-40 minutes, you will have more time in a more tranquil state. The additional time will strengthen this state's hold over your mind and body, making it a more reliable reference point to which you can return more easily.

Consider doing one longer session per week or maybe two longer sessions on weekends to maximize your time. avoid overloading yourself with tasks that become a chore. Extend your time as your innate appetite grows stronger.

3. In addition to increasing the total time, you can increase the amount of time you spend working in a particular energy center. For instance, you can find it effortless to concentrate on the center of your brain but more difficult to concentrate on your heart or

lower abdomen. It's normal to have one or more of these centers easier to concentrate on than others.

When you first begin training, you will have a natural desire to spend more time in the energy center(s) with which you are most familiar. That is perfectly acceptable; as it will help you develop your faith.

You can make the most progress in your practice and life if you spend additional time concentrating on the energy center(s). You experience the least sensation or encounter the most difficulty. These are most definitely the points in your energy flow where it is less elastic and free. These areas may hold long-held feelings or traumas.

Spending more time with these locations with an open mind, an appreciation for the way your body protects you, and relaxed observing attention will help to relieve these retained tensions, allowing your energy system to operate more completely and integrate more profoundly.

One way to accomplish this is to focus your attention in the center of every energy center on a sense of spacious, quiet stillness. Simply being present inside an energy center, resting your focus there without attempting to do something or create anything, can be therapeutic.

When beginning your practice in the Daoist tradition, it is considered prudent to concentrate extra attention on your lower dantian or lower abdominal energy core.

As energy accumulates in that core, it naturally flows upward to the middle dantian or Heart Center and the upper dantian or Mind Center. If you follow the progression or modify it to fit your needs, it's a good idea to begin and end your practice by gathering energy in your lower dantian.

4. To maintain high fertility in your lower dantian, take good care of your body. It takes surplus energy to maintain a laser-like emphasis on your practice and expand it. The foundation of this extra energy is your physical vitality. Track the following five factors to improve your physical vitality:

A. Maintain an organized "To Do" list.

B. Get enough sleep,

C. Consume a range of foods that are as fresh and natural as possible.

D. Drink enough water to remain hydrated (for most of us, roughly 64 ounces a day) and

E. Maintain a daily exercise regimen

If you've committed to waking up early to practice but are tired from your daily activities, haven't slept enough, haven't eaten well, haven't hydrated well, and haven't exercised sufficiently, you're unlikely to have the stamina for a productive practice session.

With ample physical vitality, you will devote significant attention to activating, opening, clearing, and integrating your energy centers.

5. To unlock and clear every energy center, imagine and feel yourself breathing through it. When you inhale, visualize and feel as though your breath is filling the energy source.

When you exhale, visualize and feel yourself emphasizing the emptying of the energy center and the release of any stress held there. Consider thinking that your breath is bringing light, openness, and spaciousness into your energy core when you inhale. Consider that as you exhale, you are exhaling some congestion or density.

Also, you can use this technique to relieve discomfort in any part of your body. First, visualize and feel yourself breathing into the space surrounding the restricted area, softening its edges.

Then direct your breath directly into the middle of the area where you are experiencing discomfort or tightness. Consider and sound as though your breath is infusing the region with light, openness, and spaciousness. Exhale some density or constriction.

6. Also, you should devote additional time to examining the relations between the energy centers. The Central Channel or Middle Mai Channel connects the three dantians.

This channel can be visualized and felt like a vertical cylinder stretching from your perineum (between your genitals and anus) up through your body's middle (in front of your neck but you can also picture it including the spine) to the top of your head. This channel binds and balances your three dantians.

You may have the sensation that one of your energy centers is solid, open, and clear, while another is numb, tense, or clouded. You can visualize and feel their link through the Central Channel as a way to unlock and clear the clouded core. Also, when you inhale and exhale, you can visualize and feel the breath moving between the two.

Another possibility is that you experience openness inside the energy centers themselves but not within them. You will have the impression that they are not vertically aligned or do not work well together.

For instance, your mind is not communicating with your heart or body. They are out of step. Your mind may believe one thing, while your heart may feel another and your body may crave something entirely different.

If this is the case, you can visualize and feel the Central Channel as a straight vertical column with the three dantians at its middle and breathe through it. This is something I like to do periodically during my practice to re-energize my concentration.

Also, I conclude my practice by repeatedly inhaling up through the Central Channel and exhaling down through the Central Channel. Then, before opening my eyes, I gather energy in the lower dantian.

The bottom line with energy meditation practice is that it is unique to each individual. You begin by mastering the proper form. If you've mastered the forms, you can adapt them to your unique circumstances and circumstances at any given time.

The more you comprehend the practice and develop sensitivity to your internal energy flow or lack thereof, the more you can understand how to proceed—energy meditation trains you to be more receptive to your inner guidance.

7. Once you've mastered a particular style or style of meditation using directed audio, you may wish to practice on your own without the audio. This may occur after months or even years of practice.

Allow your inner guidance to direct you to the best methods for refining and developing your internal energy. Spend additional time where it is necessary, use your breathing to release stress in specific locations, and allow your conscious presence within your energy field to guide you.

Recognize and understand when your mind wanders and gently bring it back to your meditative concentration. As you stay present, embrace whatever happens and return to allowing life energy to flow freely through you, I believe you will develop a profound faith in the deeper Life Force guiding your life.

This takes us to the eighth practice tip.

8. As you sit to meditate, bring a strong and focused purpose to your practice. Having a compelling "why" would result in unwavering concentration and attention. For instance, my goal is to become a clear conduit for Life Energy to flow through me during meditation. This is what I refer to as a Core Energy State.

I feel calm, transparent, liberated, purposeful, and whole in this state. When I enter life from this state, I discover that I am more aware of and attentive to what I am here to do, to my service to others at each moment. When I sit to meditate with a strong and simple purpose in mind, my practice gains strength.

Consider why you meditate and state your goal before beginning your practice. Assume if this helps to reawaken your drive and bolster your concentration. I hope the eight guidelines above prove beneficial in developing your meditative experience, refining your life energy, and increasing optimistic feelings of vitality and purpose in your life.

Energy Meditation Will Help You Improve Your Health, Happiness, and Success

Energy psychology and energy therapy are gaining popularity as self-development and spiritual growth methods. In India and China, an energetic perspective has been studied for over 3000 years. Today, the research has been expanded to include modern physics and biology.

It is now widely recognized in both the East and the West and acknowledged that "everything is energy." All is electricity, from the machine on which I am typing to the cells in our bodies to the thoughts and feelings we entertain.

Why is this critical?

A more energetic understanding of life reveals that our universe is much more complex and adaptable than previously believed. Rather than being composed of "immobile, inflexible matter" decided solely by material forces, our universe is composed of vibrating energetic possibilities. Our genes and brain chemistry do not entirely dictate our lives.

The energy essence of reality enables us to form our life experiences actively. Most significantly, conscious elements (intention, thinking, feeling, and belief) are among the most potent forces in this energetic reality.

According to Dr. Bruce Lipton, awareness, which includes our ideas about what is true and possible, has up to 100 times the ability to influence our well-being as any "material" force, such as medications or surgery.

Energy meditation is exemplified by Core Energy Meditation(TM). By interacting with your energy system, this activity teaches you how to master the inner technology of consciousness. To comprehend how this is possible, let us delve a little deeper into the essence of electricity.

Consider the smallest units of matter as swirling energy tornadoes or consider the fact in terms of energetic wave interactions. Our perception of these energetic forces gives them the appearance of being solid.

Many of our observations of physical processes reveal representations of reality's wave-like nature. An EKG readout visualizes the heart rate as a waveform. An EEG reveals the wave-like patterns of your brain's electrical activity. An audio mixer provides a visual representation of the sound waves. When these patterns are viewed closely, they exhibit amplitude, frequency, clarity, and coherence.

Amplitude refers to the amplitude or intensity of a wave pattern. The amplitude of a strong heartbeat or a loud sound is high. Consider amplitude in terms of energetic power or the magnitude of the effect a wave may have on its surroundings. By engaging in energetic meditation, you can bolster your energetic vibration, allowing it to have a greater impact on your life and the world around you.

Frequency is a term that refers to the number of wave cycles in a unit of time. It is a parameter that indicates the consistency of a wave-like vibration. In sound waves, you can observe the various properties of different frequencies.

A low-frequency note has some feel, whereas a high-frequency note has a completely different feel. When we say that a person or a place has "positive vibes" or "bad vibes," we refer to the various frequencies of different people or environments.

In energy meditation, we use the term "frequency" to refer to the emotions we produce. You will learn to transition into a state of positive emotion at will by energy meditation.

Clarity refers to an energetic system's lack of noise or interference. Consider the sound wave scenario once more. When the ambient world is silent, a sound comes across loud and clear. When subconscious influence is effectively minimized, your energetic vibration becomes clear.

Energy meditation teaches you to concentrate on your positive energetic vibration and to let go of the tensions, negative feelings, and restricting beliefs that prevent you from realizing your full potential. You learn to silence the thoughts in your mind to hear your inner guidance.

Coherence refers to the regularity of a wave's pattern. When all of the components of a system operate in unison, the system is coherent. You will learn how to improve, purify, clear, and balance your energetic vibration so that it functions as a harmonious whole on the inside. This allows you to work optimally in the external environment as well.

To illustrate coherence in a physical system, a coherent respiratory pattern occurs when the length of your in- and out-breaths are roughly equal. The more deeply you breathe (the greater the amplitude) and the more consistently your inhalation and exhalation match (the greater the coherence), the better and more coherent the breathing pattern becomes.

A solid, consistent breathing pattern can also align your heart rate. A consistent heart rate rhythm is indicative of a healthy heart. When the heart rate is consistent, it has a beneficial effect on other wave patterns in your body, including your brain waves. Consistent heart rate patterns appear to produce consistent brain wave patterns.

This takes us to a critical point about energy's wave-like structure:

When an energy system is solid, positive, consistent, and coherent, it tends to carry the surrounding systems into a similar state of coherence. This is referred to as resonance.

When one energetic system vibrates in unison with another, this is called resonance. The Law of Attraction is founded on the principle of resonance. Allowing the Law of Attraction to work for you requires the following: When you can lift your vibration to a state of solid, positive, and consistent coherence, you can co-ordinate the structures in your body and the energies in your world.

Due to your existence's energetic nature, you have an incredible opportunity to actively enter the energetic matrix of your life and change your experience. Core Energy Meditation(TM) enables you to do that.

Consider Doing This Simple Energy Meditation

The following meditation technique will assist you in becoming more connected to the intangible force that surrounds you and tapping into your inner psyche, referred to as imagination.

Sit or lounge in a position that is comfortable for you.

For a few minutes, close your eyes and take some deep breaths.

When inhaling deeply, think about positive thoughts that will infuse your psyche with positive energy, such as being thankful for what you have, thanking the Universe for keeping you alive, and so forth. Now consider that everything is made up of energy: the room you are in, the chair or floor you are lying or sitting on, the food you just ate, and so forth.

Consider that all of these things transform into an energy field that will gradually morph into a large area of energy surrounding you. It can be white light or another hue to assist you. After your surroundings have transformed into electricity, visualize yourself becoming one with energy. Your body is dissolving and merging with the energy you are sensing.

Once you've done this, you should feel calm and as though you've returned to your source, house, or wherever you believe your origins lie on the highest plane.

This inner tranquility you are experiencing is the purest form of consciousness. You've obliterated not only your surroundings but also yourself. This also applies to the ego. Since you are fundamentally one with the universe and the world is fundamentally one with you.

Maintain this state of energy and inner harmony for approximately 20-30 minutes.

If you have achieved complete harmony, imagine that your energetic surroundings revert to their original state and that all the melting energy has returned to the physical. This is your deliberate return to the universe.

If you become aware of your location, remain silent for a few minutes before slowly opening your eyes.

Thus, the meditation concludes.

Thus starts true self-awareness concerning the world.

CONCLUSION

It is always prudent to maintain a sense of groundedness and to replenish yourself with love and light once you are done. Opening the third eye chakra is a strenuous process that can leave you completely depleted at times. It broadens your vision, helps you comprehend more profoundly, and helps you interpret things more.

By profession, I am a qualified numerologist. I desired to experience the advantages of numerology personally. As it happens, the blissful feeling and enlightening awareness that I gained by opening my mind compelled me to continue searching. I came across chakra healing.

I am overjoyed by my newly acquired ability to perceive. It enables me to see things more clearly and to recognize what is right and wrong on an intuitive level. It's as if an intuitive compass has been implanted inside me, a compass that guides me in the right direction. I am mindful of how to achieve my objectives and of the repercussions of my decisions. I wouldn't have it any other way.

While it may seem that opening the third eye chakra would make you feel as though you are carrying the world on your shoulders, this is not the case. It is completely liberating. I now understand what I need to do and how to do it.

Today, I can use my numerology ability to benefit those around me. Healing my third eye chakra has endowed me with incredible abilities and a magnetic presence. My efforts have been rewarded and I have developed a passion for numerology.

From business tycoons to royal families, influential leaders, healing doctors, film stars, professional athletes, and everyday citizens, my balanced chakra has helped me assist these individuals in achieving their desired outcome: regaining a sense of equilibrium in their lives.

When someone asks me if they should try chakra healing or how the third eye chakra can benefit them, my response is always the same: "I am not asking you to change your life; I am simply asking you to live it; completely." That is how chakra balance aided me and it will aid you as well.

Third, eye meditation is a very simple technique to grasp. A spot on your forehead, above your nose, and between your brows is often referred to as the "third eye." Third, eye meditation focuses your attention on that point by focused visualization.

The objective is to guide chi or prana to a dormant chakra or energy core located directly beneath that location. When the third eye opens, we mean that you have made a preliminary attempt at third-eye meditation.

In this place, you usually visualize a small diamond, silver flame, white moon, a Sanskrit letter, a Hebrew letter, a Buddha, or some other auspicious silverish or bright white figure.

The theory is that when you focus on a point within or outside of your body, your body's chi energies will gravitate toward that location. Since your body's chi or natal energy flows to a specific point, it will assemble in that region and the congregation will open up the chi channels and chakras in that region due to friction.

Consider another straightforward example. You can imagine every bone in your body by imagining its form and color to be bright white. With time and continued practice, you will be able to direct your body's chi or energy to the bone. This sometimes results in the bone appearing to glow inside your

subconscious.

Also, by transmitting energy to a bone in this manner, you will eradicate illness and pain. If you have arthritis, this sometimes alleviates pain in a troublesome place. All you have to do in your visualization practice is focus on a region within the body and direct the body's physical energy to amass at that location.

When it comes to the third eye area, you are performing the same role. Why would you want to do this in the third eye region? This is because the third eye is the site of a chakra known as the two-petaled "Ajna" chakra in the body.

This is a significant upper termination point for the chi channels (acupuncture meridians) that run across the body from the perineum to the front of the head. When you direct your attention to that point due to the visualization, you will naturally send chi to that location, which will assist in opening the chakra in that region.

It is very common for people to acquire minor psychic abilities due to practicing the technique. In Anthroposophy, for example, practitioners often imagine the stages of seed germination at this point to assist in chakra opening.

Many people are advised to visualize a bright image at this stage, inside their throats, behind their breastbones, and in their bellies, in Tibetan Buddhism. Many spiritual schools teach related visualization techniques for chakra opening.